Empowering Growth - Using Proficiency Scales for Equitable and Meaningful Assessment

Quick Reads for Busy Educators

Cheryl Angst

Published by Cheryl Angst, 2023.

While every precaution has been taken in the preparation of this book, the publisher assumes no responsibility for errors or omissions, or for damages resulting from the use of the information contained herein.

EMPOWERING GROWTH - USING PROFICIENCY SCALES FOR EQUITABLE AND MEANINGFUL ASSESSMENT

First edition. June 4, 2023.

Copyright © 2023 Cheryl Angst.

ISBN: 979-8223281177

Written by Cheryl Angst.

Also by Cheryl Angst

Quick Reads for Busy Educators

Gamifying Education - How to Engage and Motivate Students Through Games

Unlocking Gamification - Exploring the Impact and Importance in Education

Winning in the Classroom - Using Bartle's Gaming Styles to Empower Learners

Who Packed Your Parachute? Why Multiple Attempts on Assessments Matter

The Power of Discussion - A Guide to Using Literature Circles in the Classroom

Together We Teach - Transforming Education Through Co-Teaching

Mentorship 101 - Your Guide to Mentoring Student Teachers with Confidence

Empowering Growth - Using Proficiency Scales for Equitable and Meaningful Assessment

Table of Contents

Introduction

AS EDUCATORS, WE HAVE the power and responsibility to create learning environments that support the growth, development, and achievement of all learners. To truly meet the diverse needs of our students, it is imperative that we adopt assessment and grading practices that are fair, accurate, and equitable.

This book is a comprehensive guide to understanding and implementing proficiency scales and equitable grading in our classrooms and educational institutions. It is a call to action, urging us to shift our mindset and practices, to reevaluate traditional grading systems, and to embrace a more student-centered and inclusive approach to assessment.

In the pages ahead, we will explore the fundamental concepts, practical strategies, and transformative potential of proficiency scales and equitable grading. We will delve into the research and principles that underpin these practices, and we will provide you with the tools and insights necessary to navigate this paradigm shift in assessment.

As we embark on this exploration of proficiency scales and equitable grading, let us remember that our ultimate goal is to create learning environments that honor the unique strengths, abilities, and experiences of every student. Together, we can build a more inclusive and empowering educational system that nurtures the growth, potential, and success of all learners.

Join us on this journey as we unravel the transformative power of proficiency scales and equitable grading. Let us embrace this opportunity to redefine assessment practices, promote fairness and equity, and unlock the true potential within our students.

Are you ready to embark on this transformative journey?

Let's begin.

Chapter 1: Understanding Proficiency Scales

I VIVIDLY REMEMBER the moment when proficiency scales revolutionized my understanding of assessment. I was reviewing a stack of graded assignments, feeling disheartened by the traditional letter grades that failed to capture the true growth and potential of my students. I knew there had to be a better way.

By luck, or by fate, I attended a professional development workshop later that week. The topic? Proficiency scales. My mind was blown – this was exactly what I needed to show student growth and learneing that letter grades just didn't accurately represent!

Implementing proficiency scales in my classroom breathed new life into my teaching practice. It enabled me to set clear learning targets and communicate them effectively to my students. No longer were they bound by arbitrary grades; instead, they were empowered to focus on their individual growth and progress towards proficiency.

I witnessed the profound impact of proficiency scales on my students' motivation and engagement. They began to take ownership of their learning, striving to reach the next level of proficiency rather than chasing a superficial grade. The scales provided them with a sense of purpose and direction, guiding their efforts and helping them understand the specific steps required for improvement.

Moreover, proficiency scales fostered a culture of continuous growth and learning. They allowed me to provide targeted feedback and personalized support to each student, tailoring my instruction to meet their specific needs. The scales facilitated meaningful conversations about progress, challenges, and next steps, promoting a collaborative and student-centered learning environment.

Understanding proficiency scales opened my eyes to the true potential of assessment as a tool for growth and development. It transformed my classroom into a space where every student's progress was valued, celebrated, and nurtured. The power of proficiency scales lies not only in their ability to capture the complexity of learning but also in their capacity to inspire students to reach new heights of achievement.

IN THIS CHAPTER, WE embark on a journey to explore the concept of proficiency scales in depth. We will uncover their benefits, delve into their design, and discover how they can revolutionize your approach to assessment.

1.1 Exploring the Concept of Proficiency

ASSESSMENT PLAYS A crucial role in measuring students' learning and growth. In recent years, there has been a growing emphasis on adopting proficiency-based assessment practices to provide a clearer understanding of students' skills and knowledge. This section examines the concept of proficiency, highlighting its significance in promoting meaningful learning and equitable assessment practices.

Understanding Proficiency

Proficiency can be defined as a level of competency or mastery in a specific domain or skill. It goes beyond traditional grading systems that focus solely on performance relative to peers. Proficiency-based assessment shifts the focus to what students can do and understand, rather than comparing them to their classmates. It enables educators to measure and communicate students' progress in relation to well-defined learning targets and standards.

The Benefits of Proficiency-based Assessment

Embracing proficiency-based assessment offers several benefits for both students and educators. Firstly, it provides clarity and transparency by clearly defining the learning expectations and criteria for proficiency. This empowers students to understand their strengths, areas for improvement, and the steps needed to reach mastery. Secondly, proficiency-based assessment promotes personalized learning by allowing students to progress at their own pace, ensuring that they have a solid foundation before advancing to more complex concepts. Additionally, it supports differentiated instruction as educators can tailor their teaching strategies to meet the unique needs of each student.

Designing Effective Proficiency Scales

To implement proficiency-based assessment successfully, educators need to develop well-crafted proficiency scales. A proficiency scale is a rubric or framework that describes the various levels of performance or understanding within a specific learning target. It outlines the specific knowledge, skills, and competencies that students must demonstrate to reach each proficiency level. Designing effective proficiency scales involves breaking down learning targets into meaningful, measurable indicators and aligning them with standards or learning outcomes. It requires clear descriptors that capture the progression from novice to expert levels of performance, allowing for accurate assessment and feedback.

Exploring the concept of proficiency in assessment opens up new possibilities for promoting meaningful learning experiences and equitable evaluation practices. By shifting the focus from grades to the development of skills and knowledge, proficiency-based assessment empowers students to take ownership of their learning journey. It provides educators with a clearer understanding of students' progress and supports targeted instruction and intervention. Understanding the concept of proficiency and its implications for assessment sets the foundation for creating a more equitable and student-centered learning environment.

1.2 Benefits of Using Proficiency Scales in Assessment

PROFICIENCY SCALES offer a valuable framework for assessing student learning and providing meaningful feedback. By using proficiency scales in assessment, educators can move away from traditional grading practices and focus on measuring students' skills and knowledge against clearly defined learning targets. This section explores the benefits of using proficiency scales and highlights their impact on promoting equity, personalized learning, and student growth.

Promoting Clarity and Transparency

One of the significant benefits of using proficiency scales is the clarity and transparency they provide. Proficiency scales outline specific learning targets and describe the progression of skills and knowledge from one level to another. This allows students to understand precisely what is expected of them and what they need to do to achieve proficiency. By removing ambiguity and subjectivity, proficiency scales provide clear benchmarks for both students and educators, promoting a shared understanding of learning goals.

Supporting Personalized Learning

Proficiency scales support personalized learning by acknowledging and accommodating the diverse learning needs and paces of students. With proficiency scales, students can progress at their own rate and move from one level to the next based on their demonstrated mastery. This approach ensures that students have a solid foundation before advancing to more complex concepts. Proficiency scales also allow educators to provide targeted instruction and interventions, addressing specific areas where students may need additional support or extension.

Encouraging Growth Mindset and Self-reflection

Using proficiency scales in assessment encourages a growth mindset and fosters a culture of self-reflection among students. By emphasizing growth and improvement over grades, proficiency scales shift the focus from a fixed notion of ability to the belief that intelligence and skills can be developed with effort and practice. Students can use the proficiency scales to self-assess their progress and set goals for further growth. This promotes metacognitive skills and empowers students to take ownership of their learning.

Enhancing Equity and Fairness

Proficiency scales promote equity in assessment by focusing on mastery of skills and knowledge rather than comparing students to their peers

Traditional grading systems often disadvantage students from diverse backgrounds or those who require additional support. However, proficiency scales provide a fair and objective measurement of students' progress against well-defined criteria. This allows educators to identify and address any gaps in learning and provide targeted support to ensure equitable opportunities for success.

Improving Feedback and Instructional Practices

Proficiency scales facilitate more meaningful feedback and guide instructional practices. With proficiency scales, educators can provide specific and actionable feedback that relates directly to the learning targets and the different proficiency levels. This helps students understand their strengths, areas for improvement, and the next steps in their learning journey. Additionally, proficiency scales assist educators in designing instruction that aligns with the various levels of proficiency, ensuring that students receive targeted and differentiated support.

The benefits of using proficiency scales in assessment are numerous and impactful. From promoting clarity and transparency to supporting personalized learning and fostering a growth mindset, proficiency scales enhance the assessment process for both students and educators. As educators embrace proficiency scales, they unlock the potential for deeper understanding, personalized growth, and continuous improvement in student learning outcomes.

1.3 Designing Effective Proficiency Scales

THIS SECTION EXAMINES the process of designing effective proficiency scales, emphasizing the importance of clarity, alignment with learning targets, and meaningful differentiation. By following a systematic approach, educators can create proficiency scales that accurately measure student growth and provide valuable feedback for improvement.

Clarity and Consistency

One of the key elements in designing effective proficiency scales is ensuring clarity and consistency. Proficiency scales should use clear language and provide specific descriptors for each level of proficiency.

This enables both educators and students to have a shared understanding of the criteria for mastery at each stage. It is crucial to avoid ambiguous or vague language that can lead to misinterpretation and unreliable assessment outcomes. Clear proficiency scales enhance the reliability and validity of assessment results.

Alignment with Learning Targets

An essential aspect of designing proficiency scales is aligning them closely with the learning targets or standards. The scales should reflect the progression of skills and knowledge outlined in the curriculum. By aligning proficiency scales with learning targets, educators ensure that the scales accurately represent the desired outcomes of instruction. This alignment enables educators to measure student progress against the specific knowledge and skills outlined in the curriculum, providing a comprehensive view of mastery.

Differentiation and Granularity

Effective proficiency scales should incorporate differentiation and granularity to capture the various levels of student achievement. By including multiple levels of proficiency, educators can recognize incremental progress and provide targeted feedback. Differentiation allows for a more nuanced understanding of student performance, enabling educators to identify specific areas of strength and areas for improvement. The inclusion of detailed descriptors at each proficiency level provides a clear roadmap for student growth.

Refinement and Continuous Improvement

Proficiency scales should not be considered static documents but rather dynamic tools that evolve over time. Educators should regularly review and refine proficiency scales based on ongoing data analysis, feedback from students and colleagues, and shifts in instructional practices. Continuous improvement ensures that the proficiency scales remain relevant, accurate, and aligned with evolving educational standards and best practices.

Chapter 2: Equitable Grading – A Framework for Fair Assessment

I HAVE ALWAYS STRIVED to treat each student with fairness and respect. However, I soon realized that traditional grading practices often inadvertently perpetuated inequities and reinforced the achievement gaps that plagued our education system. It was time for a change—a change that would ensure every student had an equal opportunity to succeed and thrive.

Enter Joe Feldman's book, "Grading for Equity," a transformative framework that allowed me to critically examine my grading practices and challenge the status quo. His approach helped me understand the profound impact that grading systems can have on students' self-esteem, motivation, and future opportunities. It highlighted the need to prioritize learning over compliance, growth over grades, and fairness over biases.

Implementing the principles of equitable grading reshaped the way I assessed my students. I began to focus on the mastery of essential skills and knowledge, rather than assigning arbitrary scores. I shifted my mindset from labeling students based on their perceived ability to providing meaningful feedback and opportunities for growth. The goal became not just to evaluate performance but to support each student's development and help them reach their full potential.

Through this journey, I discovered that grading was not a one-size-fits-all approach. It required thoughtful reflection, constant self-evaluation, and a commitment to dismantling systemic biases. It demanded that I consider the unique circumstances, backgrounds, and experiences of my students, ensuring that their voices were heard and their progress valued.

IN THIS CHAPTER, WE will explore the framework of equitable grading. We will explore its principles, uncover strategies for addressing bias, and discover ways to promote fairness and inclusivity in our assessment practices.

2.1 Unpacking the Principles of Equitable Grading

GRADING PRACTICES HAVE a profound impact on student learning and achievement. In recent years, there has been a growing recognition of the need for equitable grading practices that honor students' diverse backgrounds, experiences, and abilities. This section explores the principles of grading for equity, as advocated by educational researcher Joe Feldman. By unpacking these principles, educators can transform their grading practices to promote fairness, accuracy, and student growth.

Principle 1: Separate Academic Achievement from Behavior and Compliance

Grading for equity requires a clear distinction between academic achievement and non-academic factors such as behavior and compliance. Educators should focus solely on assessing students' mastery of the content and skills outlined in the curriculum, without penalizing or rewarding students for non-academic factors, such as handing work in late or always coming to class prepared. By separating these elements, educators provide a more accurate reflection of students' academic abilities and create an environment that values equitable assessment.

Principle 2: Embrace Mastery-Based Grading

Mastery-based grading emphasizes students' attainment of specific learning targets rather than their performance over time. This principle shifts the focus from accumulating points or grades to demonstrating mastery. Educators assess students' understanding of the content and skills through formative and summative assessments, providing targeted feedback and opportunities for improvement. Mastery-based grading acknowledges that learning is a journey, and students should be given the time and support needed to achieve mastery.

Principle 3: Provide Multiple Opportunities for Assessment and Revision

Equitable grading recognizes that students learn at different paces and benefit from multiple opportunities to demonstrate their understanding. By providing ongoing formative assessments, educators can gather evidence of student learning and offer timely feedback for improvement. Students should also have the opportunity to revise their work based on feedback, fostering a growth mindset and supporting continuous learning.

Principle 4: Focus on Learning Progression and Growth

Grading for equity considers students' growth and learning progression over time. Rather than comparing students to each other, educators assess individual growth by looking at students' progress from their own starting points. This principle acknowledges that students have different starting levels of knowledge and skills, and it values the progress they make along their unique learning journeys.

Principle 5: Communicate Clearly and Provide Feedback

Clear communication is essential for equitable grading. Educators should provide students and families with transparent expectations, grading criteria, and rubrics. Students should understand how their work will be assessed and what they need to do to succeed. Additionally, educators should offer meaningful feedback that supports student learning and provides guidance for improvement. Feedback should be specific, actionable, and focused on the learning targets.

2.2 Addressing Bias and Stereotypes in Assessment

ASSESSMENT PLAYS A crucial role in measuring student learning and informing instructional decisions. However, it is important to recognize that assessments can be influenced by bias and stereotypes, which can lead to inequitable outcomes for students. In this section, we will explore the impact of bias and stereotypes in assessment and discuss strategies for addressing and mitigating their effects. By promoting fairness and equity in assessment practices, educators can create an inclusive learning environment where all students have an equal opportunity to demonstrate their true abilities.

Understanding Bias and Stereotypes in Assessment

Bias refers to the systematic favoritism or prejudice toward certain individuals or groups, resulting in unfair advantages or disadvantages. Stereotypes, on the other hand, are preconceived notions or generalizations about individuals based on their membership in a particular group. Both bias and stereotypes can significantly impact assessment outcomes, leading to inaccurate judgments of students' abilities.

The Impact of Bias and Stereotypes on Assessment

Bias and stereotypes can manifest in various ways during the assessment process. For example, educators may hold implicit biases that influence their expectations and interpretations of student work. These biases can result in lower expectations for certain students or the reinforcement of stereotypes, leading to unequal treatment and limited opportunities for academic success. It is essential to acknowledge these biases and actively work to address them to ensure fair and unbiased assessments.

Strategies for Addressing Bias and Stereotypes in Assessment

- **Developing Clear Assessment Criteria:** Clearly define the criteria and standards for assessment tasks to minimize subjective judgments. Objectivity in assessment helps reduce the potential influence of bias and stereotypes.

- **Providing Diverse Examples and Contexts:** Use a variety of examples and contexts in assessment tasks that reflect the experiences and backgrounds of diverse students. This approach allows students to connect with the content and demonstrate their knowledge and skills in meaningful ways.

- **Offering Multiple Assessment Methods:** Incorporate a range of assessment methods to accommodate different learning styles and abilities. Providing diverse opportunities for students to showcase their understanding can mitigate the impact of bias and stereotypes.

- **Collaborative Assessment Practices:** Engage in collaborative assessment practices, such as peer and self-assessment, to foster student agency and ensure a more balanced and fair assessment process. Involving students in the assessment process promotes ownership of their learning and reduces the influence of bias and stereotypes.

2.3 Promoting Student Agency and Ownership in Grading

GRADING IS AN ESSENTIAL aspect of the education system, providing feedback and evaluating students' academic progress. However, traditional grading practices often overlook an important factor: student agency and ownership. In this section, we will explore the significance of promoting student agency and ownership in grading and how it can enhance student motivation, engagement, and learning outcomes. By involving students in the grading process and allowing them to take ownership of their learning, educators can create a more student-centered and empowering grading system.

Understanding Student Agency and Ownership in Grading

Student agency refers to the sense of autonomy and control that students have over their own learning. It involves actively engaging students in decision-making processes and valuing their perspectives and voices. Student ownership, on the other hand, relates to students taking responsibility for their learning, setting goals, and making choices that drive their academic progress. Both student agency and ownership play a vital role in fostering a positive and meaningful learning environment.

The Benefits of Promoting Student Agency and Ownership in Grading

- **Increased Motivation and Engagement:** When students have a sense of agency and ownership in the grading process, they become more motivated to take ownership of their learning. They are more likely to be engaged, set challenging goals, and strive for academic success.

- **Enhanced Self-Reflection and Self-Regulation:** Involving students in the grading process encourages self-reflection and self-regulation. Students gain a deeper understanding of their strengths and areas for growth, allowing them to make informed decisions about their learning and take necessary steps for improvement.

- **Improved Goal Setting and Progress Monitoring:** By engaging students in the grading process, they can actively participate in setting goals and monitoring their progress. This process promotes metacognitive skills, as students learn to assess their own performance and make adjustments to achieve their goals.

- **Empowered Decision-Making and Autonomy:** Allowing

students to have a say in the grading process empowers them to make informed decisions about their learning. They can provide input, negotiate criteria, and advocate for their achievements, fostering a sense of autonomy and responsibility for their academic journey.

Strategies for Promoting Student Agency and Ownership in Grading

- **Co-creating Grading Criteria:** Involve students in the development of grading criteria and rubrics. This process allows them to understand the expectations and align their efforts accordingly.

- **Self-Assessment and Reflection:** Encourage students to engage in self-assessment and reflection, where they assess their own work against the grading criteria and reflect on their learning progress. Provide guidance and prompts to support their self-reflection process.

- **Student-Led Conferences:** Facilitate student-led conferences where students showcase their learning, discuss their strengths and areas for improvement, and set goals for future growth. These conferences provide opportunities for students to take ownership of their learning and engage in meaningful conversations about their progress.

- **Feedback and Goal-Setting Discussions:** Engage in regular feedback and goal-setting discussions with students. Encourage them to provide self-assessment and reflect on their performance. Collaboratively set goals and action plans to foster ownership and accountability.

Promoting student agency and ownership in grading is a transformative approach that empowers students and enhances their learning experiences. By involving students in the grading process, educators can foster motivation, engagement, and self-regulation. By promoting student agency and ownership in grading, we empower students to become active participants in their educational journey.

Chapter 3: Integrating Proficiency Scales and Equitable Grading

THE MOMENT I INTEGRATED proficiency scales into my grading practices, I witnessed a remarkable transformation in my students' learning journey. It was as if a veil had been lifted, and a newfound clarity emerged in our classroom.

Before embracing proficiency scales, my grading system felt arbitrary and disconnected from the true purpose of education: learning and growth. Students were overwhelmed by percentages and letter grades that failed to capture the depth and breadth of their knowledge and skills. It was clear that something had to change.

As I delved into the principles of grading for equity, I discovered the power of proficiency scales in providing a clear roadmap for student progress. These scales defined specific learning targets, outlined performance expectations, and allowed students to understand where they stood in their learning journey. The focus shifted from "what grade did I get?" to "what skills do I need to develop?"

Integrating proficiency scales brought a sense of purpose and intentionality to our assessments. Students began to view their learning as a continuous process, rather than a final destination. They embraced the idea of growth and embraced challenges as opportunities for improvement. Mastery of skills became the goal, and students understood that grades were a reflection of their progress, not a measure of their worth.

The beauty of proficiency scales lies in their flexibility and adaptability to different subject areas and learning contexts. They provide a common language for teachers and students, enabling transparent and meaningful conversations about learning goals and progress. Students were no longer left guessing what was expected of them but instead had a clear understanding of the standards they needed to achieve.

By integrating proficiency scales with grading for equity, I witnessed a profound impact on student motivation, engagement, and self-confidence. They no longer felt defined by a single grade but were empowered by their ability to demonstrate mastery in various ways. The focus shifted from comparing themselves to their peers to celebrating individual growth and progress.

IN THIS CHAPTER, WE explore the integration of proficiency scales and equitable grading practices. We will delve into the practical strategies for aligning these two powerful frameworks, creating an assessment system that is equitable, meaningful, and fosters a culture of growth.

3.1 Aligning Proficiency Scales with Equitable Assessment Practices

IN THE PURSUIT OF EQUITABLE education, it is crucial to ensure that assessment practices are fair, unbiased, and aligned with the needs of all students. Proficiency scales provide a valuable framework for assessing student learning and growth. However, to truly promote equity, it is essential to align proficiency scales with equitable assessment practices. In this section, we will explore the significance of aligning proficiency scales with equitable assessment practices and discuss strategies to ensure fairness, inclusivity, and accuracy in the assessment process.

Understanding Equitable Assessment Practices

Equitable assessment practices involve recognizing and addressing biases, promoting inclusivity, and providing equal opportunities for all students to demonstrate their knowledge and skills. It requires educators to consider the diverse backgrounds, experiences, and strengths of their students and create assessment systems that accommodate individual needs.

Benefits of Aligning Proficiency Scales with Equitable Assessment Practices

- **Mitigating Bias:** By aligning proficiency scales with equitable assessment practices, educators can reduce the influence of biases that may negatively impact certain student groups. This ensures that assessment outcomes are based on genuine student performance rather than extraneous factors.

- **Inclusivity and Accessibility:** Equitable assessment practices prioritize the creation of assessments that are accessible to all students. By aligning proficiency scales with these practices, educators can provide accommodations, modifications, and alternative assessment methods to ensure that every student has an equal opportunity to demonstrate their understanding and skills.

- **Valid and Reliable Assessment:** Aligning proficiency scales with equitable assessment practices enhances the validity and reliability of the assessment process. It ensures that assessments accurately measure what they are intended to assess and produce consistent results, allowing educators to make informed decisions about student learning and progress.

Strategies for Aligning Proficiency Scales with Equitable Assessment Practices

- **Culturally Responsive Assessment:** Consider students' cultural backgrounds, languages, and experiences when designing assessments and interpreting proficiency levels. Incorporate culturally relevant content and examples that resonate with diverse student populations.

- **Multiple Measures of Assessment:** Use a variety of assessment methods, such as performance tasks, portfolios, projects, and student reflections, to provide multiple opportunities for students to demonstrate their knowledge and skills. This approach allows students to showcase their abilities in different ways, accommodating diverse learning styles and strengths.

- **Clear and Transparent Criteria:** Ensure that the criteria for each proficiency level are clearly defined and communicated to students. Provide examples and rubrics that explicitly outline what is expected at each level, allowing students to understand and work towards specific goals.

- **Ongoing Formative Assessment:** Implement ongoing formative assessment practices that provide continuous feedback and support for student learning. This approach allows for timely interventions and adjustments to instructional strategies based on students' progress and needs.

- **Collaboration and Reflection:** Engage in collaborative discussions and reflective practices with colleagues to critically examine assessment practices and address potential biases or inequities. Regularly review and revise proficiency scales to ensure they align with equitable assessment practices.

Aligning proficiency scales with equitable assessment practices is a crucial step towards creating a fair and inclusive learning environment.

Aligning proficiency scales with equitable assessment practices not only enhances the accuracy and fairness of assessments but also supports students' holistic development and achievement of academic success.

3.2 Rethinking Traditional Grading Methods

TRADITIONAL GRADING methods have long been the norm in educational systems, but they often fall short when it comes to promoting equity, fostering a growth mindset, and providing meaningful feedback to students. In this section, we will explore the limitations of traditional grading methods and discuss alternative approaches that can better support student learning and development. By rethinking traditional grading practices, educators can create a more inclusive and equitable assessment system that focuses on growth, mastery, and personalized feedback.

The Limitations of Traditional Grading

Traditional grading methods, such as assigning letter grades or percentages, tend to emphasize compliance and ranking rather than actual learning. They often rely on a single numerical value that does not adequately capture the complexity and depth of student understanding. Moreover, traditional grading can inadvertently perpetuate biases, discourage risk-taking, and undermine student motivation and self-esteem.

Alternative Approaches to Grading

- **Standards-Based Grading:** A standards-based grading system focuses on students' mastery of specific learning standards or competencies. Instead of assigning a single grade for an entire course or assignment, educators provide feedback and assess students' proficiency in individual standards. This approach allows for a more detailed and accurate representation of student progress and supports targeted instruction and intervention.

- **Competency-Based Grading:** Competency-based grading centers around the demonstration of specific skills and knowledge. Students are assessed on their ability to meet predetermined competency levels rather than compared to their peers. This approach encourages a growth mindset, as students are motivated to continually improve their skills and move towards mastery.

- **Narrative Feedback and Rubrics:** Moving away from traditional letter grades, educators can provide narrative feedback that highlights strengths, areas for improvement, and specific suggestions for growth. Using rubrics that clearly outline the criteria for success helps students understand their performance in relation to specific learning goals and fosters a deeper understanding of their strengths and areas for development.

- **Authentic Assessments:** Authentic assessments mirror real-world tasks and challenges, allowing students to apply their knowledge and skills in meaningful contexts. These assessments can include projects, portfolios, performances, and exhibitions that showcase students' abilities and provide opportunities for self-reflection and self-assessment.

Benefits of Rethinking Traditional Grading Methods

- **Equity and Inclusion:** Alternative grading approaches prioritize fairness and equal opportunities for all students. By focusing on individual growth and progress rather than comparison to peers, these methods reduce the impact of external factors and biases on students' grades.

- **Motivation and Engagement:** Shifting to alternative grading methods promotes intrinsic motivation and engagement in learning. By emphasizing growth, mastery, and personalized feedback, students become more actively involved in their own learning process and take ownership of their academic journey.

- **Meaningful Feedback:** Rethinking traditional grading allows educators to provide more detailed, specific, and actionable feedback to students. This feedback helps students understand their strengths and areas for improvement, supports their ongoing learning, and guides them towards targeted growth.

- **Holistic Assessment:** Alternative grading approaches consider a broader range of student abilities, talents, and intelligences. They encourage a more holistic view of student achievement by recognizing and valuing diverse forms of knowledge and skills beyond traditional academic measures.

Rethinking traditional grading methods is a vital step towards creating a more equitable and student-centered assessment system. These methods promote equity, motivation, and engagement, allowing students to develop a deeper understanding of their learning and strive for continuous improvement. By reimagining grading practices, educators can better support student success and foster a culture of lifelong learning.

3.3 Strategies for Balancing Mastery and

Growth

BALANCING THE CONCEPTS of mastery and growth is a key consideration when designing an effective assessment system. Mastery entails reaching a high level of proficiency in specific skills or knowledge, while growth focuses on continuous improvement and progress over time. In this section, we will explore strategies that educators can employ to strike a balance between these two important dimensions of learning. By combining mastery and growth-oriented approaches, educators can create a comprehensive assessment framework that promotes both depth of understanding and ongoing development.

Understanding Mastery and Growth

Mastery refers to the attainment of a high level of proficiency in a particular skill or area of knowledge. It represents a comprehensive understanding and the ability to apply concepts or skills effectively. On the other hand, growth emphasizes the ongoing progress, improvement, and learning that occurs over time. It recognizes that students have diverse starting points and can continue to develop their abilities with support and effort.

Strategies for Balancing Mastery and Growth

- **Clear Learning Objectives:** Establish clear and specific learning objectives that outline the desired level of mastery for each skill or concept. These objectives serve as benchmarks for students' progress and guide their learning journey. Ensure that the objectives allow for flexibility and growth, providing room for students to go beyond the expected level of mastery.

- **Differentiated Instruction:** Implement differentiated instruction techniques to meet students' individual needs and facilitate their growth. Provide opportunities for students to work at their own pace and offer personalized support and resources to address their unique areas of growth. Differentiation allows students to develop mastery in their own time while supporting their ongoing progress.

- **Formative Assessment:** Incorporate frequent formative assessments throughout the learning process to monitor students' growth and understanding. Formative assessments provide timely feedback, identify areas for improvement, and guide instructional decisions. They promote growth by helping students understand their current level of mastery and setting targets for future development.

- **Reflective Practices:** Encourage students to engage in reflective practices that promote self-assessment and self-regulation. Provide opportunities for students to reflect on their strengths, areas for improvement, and strategies for growth. Reflective practices foster metacognitive skills and empower students to take ownership of their learning and growth.

- **Portfolio Assessment:** Implement portfolio assessment as a means to showcase students' growth and development over time. Portfolios provide a comprehensive collection of student work, demonstrating both mastery and growth in various areas. They offer a holistic view of students' progress and provide evidence of their ongoing learning journey.

- **Feedback for Growth:** Provide constructive feedback that focuses on both mastery and growth. Celebrate students' achievements and strengths while also offering specific suggestions for improvement and areas of further development. Feedback should be timely, specific, actionable, and individualized, supporting students' ongoing growth while reinforcing their mastery of skills and knowledge.

Balancing mastery and growth in assessment is crucial for promoting both depth of understanding and ongoing development. Emphasizing both mastery and growth enables students to reach high levels of proficiency while maintaining a growth mindset and a commitment to lifelong learning. By striking this balance, educators can ensure that assessment practices empower students to achieve their full potential and thrive academically.

3.4 Proficiency Versus Percentages: What's the Big Deal?

IN THE REALM OF TRADITIONAL education, grading with percentages has long been the prevailing approach. However, this system often leads to an emphasis on failure, with a significant portion of the grading scale dedicated to failing marks. Moreover, the mathematical limitations of redeeming a failing grade under the percentage system present additional challenges. This article delves into the transformative power of proficiency scales, which offer a more equitable and redemptive alternative to the percentage-based grading system. By shifting the focus from failure to growth and providing viable pathways to success, proficiency scales promote fairness, accuracy, and student development.

Understanding the Pitfalls of the Percentage System

The percentage system is inherently flawed as it allocates a substantial portion of the grading scale to failing grades. Often, a range of 50-60 points is designated as "failing," creating a negative environment that emphasizes shortcomings rather than growth. This approach can demotivate students and hinder their progress, failing to recognize the incremental steps they make towards mastery.

The Mathematical Impossibility of Redemption

Under the percentage system, redeeming a failing grade can be an arduous task due to mathematical limitations. Suppose a student receives a failing grade of 50% on an assignment. To reach a passing grade of, let's say, 70%, the student would need to achieve a perfect score on every subsequent assignment, which is often an unrealistic expectation. This mathematical hurdle limits opportunities for growth, discourages resilience, and undermines the notion of progress.

Proficiency Scales: A Beacon of Equity and Redemption

Proficiency scales provide a compelling alternative to the percentage system by fostering a growth-oriented mindset and offering viable pathways to success. Unlike the percentage system, proficiency scales focus on students' progress and attainment of specific skills or knowledge areas. They break down complex concepts into manageable components and define clear levels of proficiency with descriptive criteria.

Equity in Assessment and Growth Mindset

Proficiency scales inherently promote equity by shifting the emphasis from failure to growth. Students are assessed based on their individual progress and mastery of specific skills, rather than being compared to others. This approach recognizes and values students' diverse talents and strengths, encouraging them to view challenges as opportunities for improvement. Feedback within the proficiency scale framework becomes constructive, actionable, and empowering, fostering intrinsic motivation and resilience.

Redemption and Pathways to Success

Unlike the percentage system, proficiency scales offer tangible opportunities for redemption and growth. With clearly defined descriptors and criteria for each level of proficiency, students can understand their current standing and the steps needed to progress. Proficiency scales provide a roadmap for improvement, allowing students to build upon their existing knowledge and skills. This ensures that every student has a fair chance to succeed and develop a sense of accomplishment.

The percentage system's focus on failure and the mathematical challenges it poses for redemption necessitate a shift towards proficiency scales. These scales provide an equitable and redemptive approach to assessment, emphasizing growth and providing viable pathways to success. By embracing proficiency scales, educators can foster a culture of resilience, intrinsic motivation, and continuous improvement.

Chapter 4: Designing Proficiency Scales

I REMEMBER THE DAYS when I struggled with the complexities of grading using percentages. I constantly found myself grappling with the question of what differences separated scores like a 72% from a 73% in an assignment. Was it one more grammatical mistake? A single spelling error? Why was my 72% different from my colleague's across the hall?. It was a convoluted process that left me feeling uncertain and detached from the true meaning of assessment.

However, my perspective transformed when I discovered the simplicity and effectiveness of grading with a proficiency scale. The clarity and purpose it brought to the evaluation process were like a breath of fresh air. Rather than fixating on arbitrary percentages, I could now focus on the essential skills and knowledge that students needed to acquire.

Using a proficiency scale eliminated the guesswork and ambiguity that plagued my previous grading methods. I no longer had to spend countless hours deciphering minute discrepancies between scores. Instead, I could assess students' progress based on clear and well-defined descriptors of proficiency levels.

The proficiency scale provided a comprehensive framework that captured the essence of student learning. It allowed me to provide meaningful feedback and guide students towards specific areas for growth. By focusing on the development of skills and competencies, rather than arbitrary numbers, I could foster a growth mindset and instill a sense of purpose in my students.

Gone were the days of assigning grades based on elusive percentages. Now, I could confidently assess and communicate student progress in a way that was transparent, fair, and aligned with their learning goals. The proficiency scale empowered me to recognize and celebrate the unique strengths and *achievements of each student, rather than reducing them to a mere numerical value.*

Grading with a proficiency scale not only simplified my assessment process, but it also transformed my classroom culture. Students became more engaged, motivated, and invested in their own learning journeys. They embraced challenges as opportunities for growth and strived to reach higher levels of proficiency.

Looking back, I am grateful for the shift to a proficiency scale. It has redefined how I assess and evaluate student progress, offering a more meaningful and equitable approach. No longer entangled in the complexities of percentages, I can focus on fostering a growth mindset and supporting my students in their quest for knowledge and mastery.

IN THIS CHAPTER, WE will examine the fundamental components of effective proficiency scales as well as how to create them. The chapter will finish with some simple examples from various subjects to help give you a jumping off point for creating your own scales. While some assessments may call for complex proficiency scales, you may find that for the most part, the simplest ones are the most effective.

4.1 Determining the Size and Granularity

WHEN CREATING A PROFICIENCY scale, it is essential to carefully consider the number of sections that will best serve your assessment goals. Here are three key considerations to guide your decision-making process:

Assess the Complexity of the Learning Target

Start by assessing the complexity of the learning target or skill you want to assess. Determine if the learning target can be adequately represented by a single scale or if it requires multiple dimensions to capture its full complexity. For example, a math proficiency scale might include sections for understanding and applying concepts, problem-solving and reasoning, and mathematical communication. Assess the level of granularity needed to accurately capture student progress and adjust the number of sections accordingly.

Consider Curriculum Scope and Sequence

Examine your curriculum's scope and sequence to identify key learning areas and milestones. Consider if these milestones can be effectively represented by separate sections in the proficiency scale. Ensure that the number of sections aligns with the breadth of the curriculum and the desired learning goals. A language proficiency scale, for instance, may include sections for listening comprehension, speaking skills, reading comprehension, and writing proficiency.

Seek Input from Colleagues and Experts

Collaboration with colleagues and subject-matter experts can provide valuable insights and perspectives. Engage in discussions and consultations to gather diverse input on the optimal number of sections for your proficiency scale. Seek the experiences and advice of educators who have successfully implemented similar scales. Their expertise can help you make informed decisions about the number of sections that will best support accurate and meaningful assessment of student growth.

By carefully considering these factors and seeking input from relevant stakeholders, you can determine the appropriate number of sections for your proficiency scale. Remember, the goal is to create a scale that effectively captures student progress and provides clear guidance for instructional planning and support.

4.2 Writing Clear and Powerful Descriptors

CREATING CLEAR AND powerful descriptors is crucial when developing a proficiency scale. Here are three key strategies to guide you in writing effective descriptors:

Understand the Purpose of Each Section

Begin by defining the purpose and desired outcomes for each section within the proficiency scale. Clearly articulate the specific knowledge, skills, or competencies to be assessed in each section. Ensure that the descriptors within each section align with the intended outcomes and accurately reflect the progression of student growth. For example, a science proficiency scale might have a section dedicated to scientific inquiry skills, with descriptors that focus on hypothesis formulation, data collection and analysis, and drawing conclusions.

Use Action Verbs and Specific Language

Utilize action verbs that clearly communicate the expected behaviors or actions of students at each proficiency level. Choose words that accurately describe the level of proficiency being assessed. Be specific and precise in your language to provide a clear understanding of what is expected. Avoid vague or ambiguous terms that could lead to misinterpretation or confusion. For instance, instead of using a general term like "understands," opt for more specific action verbs such as "analyzes," "evaluates," or "applies."

Include Clear Criteria and Examples

Provide clear criteria that define the expectations for each proficiency level within the descriptors. Clearly state the benchmarks that differentiate one proficiency level from another. Include both qualitative and quantitative indicators to support the assessment of student performance. Additionally, wherever possible, incorporate concrete examples or evidence that illustrate each descriptor. These examples can help teachers and students better understand the expected level of proficiency and serve as a reference point for assessment.

4.3 Sample Proficiency Scales

THE SIZE AND SCOPE of proficiency scales will change depending on the nature and complexity of the assessment.

For example, an assignment where the teacher is only assessing how students understand and apply mathematical concepts might have a scale that looks like this:

Novice	Developing	Proficient	Advanced
Demonstrates limited understanding and struggles to apply mathematical concepts in real-world situations.	Demonstrates partial understanding and inconsistently applies mathematical concepts in some real-world situations.	Demonstrates solid understanding and consistently applies mathematical concepts in various real-world situations.	Demonstrates deep understanding and effectively applies mathematical concepts in complex real-world situations.

However, if the teacher wanted to assess more than one criteria for this same assignment (or for a more complex assignment), the proficiency scale might look like this:

Novice	Developing	Proficient	Advanced
Demonstrates limited understanding and struggles to apply mathematical concepts in real-world situations.	Demonstrates partial understanding and inconsistently applies mathematical concepts in some real-world situations.	Demonstrates solid understanding and consistently applies mathematical concepts in various real-world situations.	Demonstrates deep understanding and effectively applies mathematical concepts in complex real-world situations.
Struggles to solve mathematical problems and lacks logical reasoning skills.	Demonstrates some problem-solving skills and applies basic reasoning in simple mathematical problems.	Applies effective problem-solving strategies and uses logical reasoning to solve a variety of mathematical problems.	Excels in problem-solving and demonstrates advanced reasoning skills in complex mathematical problems.
Struggles to express mathematical ideas and reasoning clearly and effectively.	Demonstrates some ability to communicate mathematical ideas, but with limited clarity and organization.	Communicates mathematical ideas and reasoning clearly and effectively using appropriate mathematical language.	Articulates complex mathematical ideas and reasoning with precision, clarity, and logical coherence.

Here are some simple proficiency scales for language arts assignments that could be used alone or combined to create more complex scales:

Listening Comprehension:

Novice	Developing	Proficient	Advanced
Struggles to understand simple spoken language and relies heavily on support and repetition.	Understands some familiar spoken language with support and can follow basic instructions.	Comprehends a range of spoken language, including both familiar and unfamiliar topics, with moderate support.	Demonstrates excellent listening comprehension, understanding complex spoken language with minimal support.

Speaking Skills:

Novice	Developing	Proficient	Advanced
Struggles to express basic ideas and uses limited vocabulary and grammatical structures.	Communicates with simple sentences and vocabulary, though with some errors and hesitations.	Communicates effectively using a range of vocabulary and grammatical structures, with occasional errors.	Expresses ideas fluently and accurately, demonstrating a wide-ranging vocabulary and complex sentence structures.

Reading Comprehension:

Novice	Developing	Proficient	Advanced
Struggles to understand simple written texts and relies on basic vocabulary and comprehension strategies.	Understands basic written texts on familiar topics with support and uses simple comprehension strategies.	Comprehends a variety of written texts on familiar and some unfamiliar topics with moderate support.	Demonstrates excellent reading comprehension, understanding complex texts with minimal support and applying advanced comprehension strategies.

Writing Proficiency:

Novice	Developing	Proficient	Advanced
Produces simple sentences with limited vocabulary and frequent errors.	Writes short texts on familiar topics with basic vocabulary and some errors.	Writes coherent and well-structured texts on various topics, using a range of vocabulary and grammar structures.	Produces sophisticated and well-crafted written texts, demonstrating advanced vocabulary, grammar, and organization.

The author's school district uses "Emerging", "Developing", "Proficient", and "Extending" as the descriptors for their proficiency scales. To help both students and parents understand how the scale assesses student performance, the author includes a brief descriptor from the provincial reporting document, explaining what each level represents. Here is a generic scale where the "concepts and competencies relevant to the expected learning" can be replaced with specific criteria:

Emerging	Developing	Proficient	Extending
The student demonstrates an *initial* understanding of the concepts and competencies relevant to the expected learning. "Emerging" indicates that a student is just beginning to demonstrate learning in relation to the learning standards but is not yet doing so consistently. *Emerging isn't failing.*	The student demonstrates a *partial* understanding of the concepts and competencies relevant to the expected learning. "Developing" indicates that a student is demonstrating learning in relation to the learning standards with growing consistency. The student is showing initial understanding but is still in the process of developing their competency in relation to the learning standards. *Developing isn't failing.*	The student demonstrates a *complete* understanding of the concepts and competencies relevant to the expected learning. *"Proficient" is the goal for all students.* A student is Proficient when they demonstrate the expected learning in relation to the learning standards. Proficient is not synonymous with perfection. Instead, the student is able to demonstrate their learning consistently or most of the time.	The student demonstrates a *sophisticated* understanding of the concepts and competencies relevant to the expected learning. "Extending" is not synonymous with perfection. A student is Extending when they demonstrate learning, in relation to learning standards, with increasing depth and complexity. *Extending is not a bonus or a reward.*

Chapter 5: Engaging Students in Self-Assessment and Reflection

LOOKING BACK AT MY early years as an educator, I recall a time when self-assessment and reflection were rarely on my radar. Like many teachers, I was solely focused on delivering content, assessing student work, and providing feedback. The idea of students actively engaging in their own assessment and reflecting on their learning seemed distant and unfamiliar.

It was during a professional development workshop that I had a transformative moment. The facilitator introduced the concept of self-assessment and its potential to empower students as active participants in their educational journey. Intrigued, I decided to give it a try in my own classroom.

I introduced self-assessment activities that encouraged students to reflect on their progress, identify their strengths and areas for improvement, and set meaningful goals for themselves. Initially, there was some resistance and confusion. Students were accustomed to relying on the teacher for evaluation and guidance. However, with patience, support, and modeling, they began to embrace the process.

I witnessed a remarkable shift in my students' attitudes and engagement. They took ownership of their learning, using self-assessment as a tool for self-reflection and growth. They became more aware of their strengths and areas for improvement, and actively sought strategies to overcome challenges. I saw a newfound sense of confidence and motivation in their approach to learning.

As I reflected on this experience, I realized the immense value of engaging students in self-assessment and reflection. It not only fosters a deeper understanding of their own learning, but also cultivates essential skills such as critical thinking, metacognition, and self-regulation. It empowers students to become active participants in their educational journey, shaping their own path to success.

IN THIS CHAPTER, WE delve into the power of engaging students in self-assessment and reflection. We explore practical strategies, tools, and activities that will enable you to foster a classroom culture of self-reflection and metacognition.

5.1 Empowering Students Through Self-Assessment

IN THE JOURNEY OF PROFICIENCY-based assessment, empowering students to take ownership of their learning is crucial for their growth and development. Self-assessment is a powerful tool that promotes student agency, metacognition, and reflection. By actively engaging students in assessing their own progress and setting learning goals, educators can foster a culture of self-directed learning and empower students to become lifelong learners. In this section, we explore the benefits and strategies for empowering students through self-assessment.

The Benefits of Self-Assessment

Self-assessment offers several benefits to students, including:

- **Ownership of Learning:** When students assess their own progress, they become active participants in their learning journey. They take responsibility for their strengths and areas for growth, allowing them to set meaningful goals and develop strategies to achieve them.

- **Metacognitive Development:** Self-assessment encourages students to reflect on their thinking, learning processes, and strategies. By examining their strengths and weaknesses, students gain a deeper understanding of their own learning styles and preferences, leading to improved metacognitive skills.

- **Goal Setting and Personalized Learning:** Through self-assessment, students learn to set realistic and meaningful goals based on their individual needs. They develop a sense of purpose and direction, tailoring their learning experiences to match their interests and aspirations.

- **Increased Motivation and Engagement:** When students are actively involved in assessing their own progress, they become more motivated and engaged in their learning. Self-assessment provides a sense of ownership and autonomy, fostering a positive learning environment.

Strategies for Empowering Students through Self-Assessment

- **Clear Learning Targets:** Ensure that students have a clear understanding of the learning targets or outcomes. Provide rubrics, exemplars, or checklists that outline the criteria for success. This clarity helps students evaluate their work against specific criteria.

- **Reflection and Self-Evaluation:** Incorporate regular opportunities for students to reflect on their learning. Use prompts or guiding questions that encourage them to assess their strengths, areas for growth, and progress toward their goals. Encourage them to provide evidence or examples to support their self-evaluation.

- **Goal Setting:** Guide students in setting realistic and challenging goals based on their self-assessment. Help them develop action plans and strategies to achieve their goals. Regularly revisit these goals and provide support and feedback as needed.

- **Peer and Collaborative Assessment:** Engage students in peer assessment and collaborative discussions. Encourage them to provide feedback to their peers and engage in constructive dialogue to deepen their understanding of the assessment criteria and learning targets.

- **Reflective Journals or Portfolios:** Incorporate reflective journals or digital portfolios where students can document their learning journey, showcase their progress, and reflect on their achievements and challenges. Encourage students to regularly review their entries and make connections between their self-assessment and growth over time.

- **Teacher-Student Conferences:** Schedule one-on-one conferences with students to discuss their self-assessments, goals, and progress. Provide feedback, ask probing questions, and offer guidance to support their self-assessment process.

These conferences help build a trusting relationship and promote personalized support.

Empowering students through self-assessment is a transformative approach to assessment that fosters student agency, metacognitive skills, and lifelong learning. By involving students in the assessment process, educators create a culture of self-reflection, goal setting, and continuous improvement.

5.2 Promoting Metacognition and Reflection Skills

METACOGNITION AND REFLECTION are essential cognitive processes that empower students to become active, self-directed learners. By promoting metacognitive awareness and providing opportunities for reflection, educators can enhance students' ability to monitor, regulate, and evaluate their own thinking and learning. In this section, we explore the significance of metacognition and reflection in education and discuss strategies to foster these crucial skills in students.

The Importance of Metacognition and Reflection

Metacognition refers to the awareness and understanding of one's own cognitive processes, including thinking, learning, and problem-solving. Reflection, on the other hand, involves the deliberate and thoughtful consideration of experiences, actions, and outcomes. Both metacognition and reflection play vital roles in students' cognitive and emotional development, enabling them to:

- **Monitor and Regulate Learning:** Metacognition allows students to monitor their understanding, identify gaps in knowledge, and regulate their learning strategies. They can adjust their approach, seek clarification, or seek additional resources to improve their understanding and mastery of concepts.

- **Develop Critical Thinking Skills:** Metacognition encourages students to think deeply about their thinking. It promotes critical thinking by enabling them to analyze and evaluate their reasoning processes, biases, and assumptions. Students become more aware of their cognitive biases, leading to more balanced and objective thinking.

- **Enhance Problem-Solving Abilities:** Metacognition equips students with problem-solving skills by enabling them to identify and apply appropriate strategies, evaluate their effectiveness, and adjust their approach as needed. They become more adept at identifying patterns, making connections, and applying their knowledge to new situations.

- **Foster Self-Regulated Learning:** Metacognitive and reflective practices help students become self-regulated learners who can set goals, plan their learning, manage their time effectively, and evaluate their progress. They develop a sense of ownership and responsibility for their learning.

Strategies to Promote Metacognition and Reflection

- **Explicitly Teach Metacognitive Strategies:** Introduce students to metacognitive strategies such as think-alouds, self-questioning, concept mapping, and journaling. Teach them how to monitor their understanding, identify gaps, and regulate their learning.

- **Provide Reflection Prompts and Tools:** Offer structured reflection prompts or journaling activities that encourage students to reflect on their learning experiences, challenges, and achievements. These prompts could include questions like "What did I learn?" or "How can I apply this knowledge to real-life situations?"

- **Scaffold Reflection Activities:** Gradually increase the complexity of reflection activities, providing scaffolding and support as needed. Begin with simple prompts and gradually introduce more open-ended and thought-provoking questions that require deeper reflection and analysis.

- **Encourage Metacognitive Discussions:** Foster metacognitive discussions among students by incorporating collaborative activities, group projects, and peer feedback sessions. Encourage students to share their thoughts, perspectives, and problem-solving strategies, promoting metacognitive awareness.

- **Model Metacognitive Thinking:** Model metacognitive thinking by verbalizing your own thinking processes, demonstrating how to approach complex tasks, and discussing problem-solving strategies. Show students how to reflect on challenges, evaluate different perspectives, and make informed decisions.

- **Provide Feedback on Metacognition and Reflection:** Provide specific and constructive feedback on students' metacognitive processes and reflective activities. Recognize their growth, offer guidance for improvement, and encourage them to set new goals based on their reflections.

By fostering metacognitive awareness, students develop the ability to monitor and regulate their learning, enhance their problem-solving abilities, and become self-directed learners. These skills are essential for students' long-term success and equip them with the tools to navigate complex challenges and become lifelong learners.

5.3 Peer Assessment and Collaborative Reflection

PEER ASSESSMENT AND collaborative reflection are powerful strategies that promote active learning, foster a sense of ownership, and enhance students' metacognitive and reflective abilities. By engaging students in assessing their peers' work and engaging in reflective discussions, educators can create an environment that encourages collaboration, critical thinking, and self-improvement. In this section, we explore the benefits of peer assessment and collaborative reflection and discuss effective strategies for implementing these practices in the classroom.

The Benefits of Peer Assessment

Peer assessment offers several benefits to students, including:

- **Constructive Feedback:** Engaging in peer assessment allows students to provide and receive feedback from their peers. This process promotes the development of critical thinking skills, as students learn to evaluate and provide constructive feedback on their peers' work. They gain insights into different perspectives and approaches, fostering a deeper understanding of the subject matter.

- **Active Learning:** Peer assessment encourages students to actively engage with the content and criteria of the assessment. When assessing their peers' work, students must carefully evaluate the quality, relevance, and effectiveness of the work, promoting deeper comprehension and analysis.

- **Collaboration and Communication:** Peer assessment promotes collaboration and communication skills as students discuss and exchange ideas, justify their evaluations, and provide suggestions for improvement. It enhances their ability to articulate their thoughts and engage in respectful and constructive dialogue.

- **Self-Reflection:** Through assessing the work of their peers, students gain a clearer understanding of their own strengths and areas for improvement. They learn to apply the same evaluative criteria to their own work, enhancing their self-reflection skills and enabling them to set goals for growth.

Strategies for Effective Peer Assessment

- **Clear Guidelines and Criteria:** Provide students with clear guidelines and criteria for the assessment. Clearly communicate the expectations, evaluation criteria, and standards to ensure consistency and fairness in the assessment process.

- **Training in Assessment Skills:** Before engaging in peer assessment, provide students with explicit instruction on assessment skills, such as providing constructive feedback, using descriptive language, and offering specific suggestions for improvement. Model and scaffold the process to help students develop these skills effectively.

- **Peer Feedback Protocols:** Establish structured protocols for peer feedback to ensure that students provide constructive and meaningful feedback. These protocols can include guidelines on how to deliver feedback respectfully, focus on strengths, and provide actionable suggestions for improvement.

- **Reflection and Discussion:** Incorporate reflection and discussion activities following peer assessment. Encourage students to reflect on their own work, consider the feedback received from their peers, and identify areas for growth. Facilitate collaborative discussions where students can share their feedback, discuss different perspectives, and collectively reflect on their learning.

- **Peer Accountability:** Foster a sense of accountability by emphasizing the importance of taking the assessment process seriously and respecting the effort and time invested by their peers. Encourage students to be responsible assessors and supportive peers throughout the process.

Collaborative Reflection

- **Group Reflection Activities:** Engage students in group reflection activities where they can discuss their learning experiences, insights gained, and challenges faced. This promotes collaborative learning and allows students to benefit from each other's perspectives and experiences.

- **Structured Reflection Prompts:** Provide structured reflection prompts that guide students in reflecting on their learning process, the effectiveness of their strategies, and areas for improvement. These prompts can encourage students to think critically, analyze their learning journey, and set goals for future growth.

- **Collaborative Problem-Solving:** Encourage students to work together in solving complex problems and reflecting on their problem-solving strategies. This collaborative reflection allows students to evaluate the effectiveness of different approaches, consider alternative solutions, and learn from each other's insights.

- **Peer-led Reflection Discussions:** Assign students the role of facilitators in reflection discussions, allowing them to lead and guide the conversation. This empowers students to take ownership of their learning and develop leadership and communication skills.

Peer assessment and collaborative reflection are valuable tools for promoting active learning, critical thinking, and self-improvement among students. By incorporating these strategies in the classroom, educators can create an environment that fosters collaboration, deepens understanding, and empowers students to become self-directed learners.

Chapter 6: Addressing Challenges and Overcoming Obstacles

SWITCHING FROM PERCENTAGES to proficiency scales was a significant change in my classroom, but it didn't come without its challenges. I faced resistance from both parents and colleagues who were accustomed to the traditional grading system.

Parents were concerned about the unfamiliarity of proficiency scales and how they would understand their child's progress. Some questioned the lack of exact percentages and worried that it might hinder college applications or future opportunities.

Colleagues, too, expressed doubts and hesitations. They were comfortable with the old ways of grading and were unsure about the effectiveness and validity of proficiency scales. Some feared the additional workload in creating and implementing the new system.

However, I was determined to help them see the value and benefits of proficiency scales. I organized parent information sessions and provided clear explanations of the scale's purpose, emphasizing its focus on growth and mastery rather than a single numerical value. I addressed their concerns and showcased examples of how proficiency scales offered a more accurate representation of their child's progress.

With my colleagues, I initiated conversations and shared research and success stories from other educators who had already implemented proficiency scales. We collaborated on developing consistent descriptors and aligned our expectations to ensure a smooth transition.

Over time, resistance started to diminish. Parents and colleagues began to appreciate the equity and clarity that proficiency scales brought to the assessment process. They saw how it supported student growth, provided targeted feedback, and encouraged a growth mindset.

Switching from percentages to proficiency scales was not an easy journey, but it was a necessary one. By addressing concerns, fostering understanding, and highlighting the benefits, I was able to overcome resistance and create a more meaningful and equitable grading system in my classroom.

In this chapter, we will delve into the world of addressing challenges and overcoming obstacles in education. We will explore strategies for identifying and understanding the diverse challenges students may face, and we will discuss practical approaches for creating inclusive and supportive learning environments. From fostering resilience and grit to collaborating with colleagues and families, we will explore the tools and techniques that can help us navigate the path to success.

6.1 Navigating Resistance and Overcoming Barriers

IN THE JOURNEY OF IMPLEMENTING new approaches to assessment and grading, educators often encounter resistance and face various barriers. In this section, we explore the challenges that may arise when implementing proficiency-based assessment and grading practices and provide strategies for navigating resistance and overcoming barriers. By understanding the underlying reasons for resistance and employing effective strategies, educators can successfully navigate these obstacles and create a supportive environment that embraces equitable assessment practices.

Understanding Resistance

Resistance to change is a natural response, and it can manifest in different forms when introducing proficiency-based assessment and grading. Some common sources of resistance include:

- **Familiarity with Traditional Practices:** Educators and stakeholders may be comfortable with traditional grading practices and feel uncertain about the shift to proficiency-based approaches. They may resist change due to a fear of the unknown or concerns about the effectiveness of the new methods.

- **Perceived Loss of Control:** Resistance may arise when educators feel that proficiency-based assessment reduces their autonomy in determining student grades. They may worry that it limits their professional judgment or reduces flexibility in addressing individual student needs.

- **Parental and Community Expectations:** Some parents and community members may have expectations based on traditional grading systems, making them resistant to changes that differ from what they are accustomed to. Addressing their concerns and providing clear communication is crucial in navigating this form of resistance.

Strategies for Navigating Resistance

- **Communicate the Rationale:** Clearly communicate the benefits and purpose of proficiency-based assessment and grading practices to all stakeholders. Explain how it supports student learning, promotes equitable opportunities, and provides a more accurate reflection of student proficiency.

Address concerns and answer questions to alleviate fears and misconceptions.

- **Provide Professional Development:** Offer professional development opportunities for educators to develop a deep understanding of proficiency-based assessment practices. Provide training on the underlying principles, implementation strategies, and evidence supporting the effectiveness of these approaches. This will help build confidence and competence among educators.

- **Involve Stakeholders in the Process:** Engage key stakeholders, such as teachers, administrators, parents, and students, in the decision-making process. Seek their input, involve them in planning and implementation, and address their concerns and perspectives. This collaborative approach fosters a sense of ownership and encourages buy-in.

- **Start with Small Steps:** Introduce proficiency-based assessment gradually, starting with small changes and pilot programs. This allows educators and students to become familiar with the new practices and experience success, which can build confidence and support broader implementation.

- **Provide Ongoing Support:** Offer ongoing support and professional learning opportunities as educators navigate the transition. Provide resources, mentoring, and coaching to help educators implement proficiency-based practices effectively. Regularly assess and address any challenges or concerns that arise.

Overcoming Barriers

- **Lack of Resources:** Address resource constraints by seeking external funding, leveraging partnerships, and advocating for necessary resources. This may include technology tools, professional development opportunities, or materials to support proficiency-based assessment.

- **Alignment with Existing Systems:** Identify areas of alignment between proficiency-based assessment practices and existing policies and systems. Highlight how these new approaches can complement and enhance existing practices, rather than replace them entirely.

- **Addressing Equity Concerns:** Be proactive in addressing equity concerns that may arise during the implementation process. Ensure that proficiency-based assessment practices do not perpetuate biases or disadvantage certain student groups. Provide training and support to educators on culturally responsive assessment practices and bias mitigation.

6.2 Sustaining Equitable Assessment Practices Over Time

IMPLEMENTING EQUITABLE assessment practices is a transformative journey that requires ongoing commitment and dedication. In this chapter, we delve into the importance of sustaining equitable assessment practices over time and explore strategies for ensuring their continued effectiveness. By fostering a culture of equity, providing professional development opportunities, and cultivating a reflective and adaptive mindset, educators can create a sustainable framework for equitable assessment.

Creating a Culture of Equity

Sustaining equitable assessment practices begins with cultivating a culture of equity within the educational community. This involves promoting awareness, understanding, and buy-in from all stakeholders, including administrators, teachers, students, and parents. Key strategies for creating a culture of equity include:

- **Professional Learning Communities:** Foster collaborative spaces where educators can engage in discussions, share experiences, and collectively explore strategies to promote equitable assessment practices. Encourage regular meetings and opportunities for professional development focused on equity in assessment.

- **School-wide Policies:** Establish clear policies that promote equity in assessment and grading across all classrooms. Ensure consistency in expectations and practices, while allowing for flexibility to meet individual student needs.

- **Student Involvement:** Engage students in the conversation about equitable assessment practices. Encourage their input, provide opportunities for self-reflection, and empower them to take ownership of their learning journey.

Providing Ongoing Professional Development

Sustaining equitable assessment practices requires continuous professional development for educators. This ensures that they stay updated with research, best practices, and emerging trends in equitable assessment. Strategies for providing ongoing professional development include:

- **Workshops and Training:** Offer regular workshops, seminars, and training sessions focused on equity in assessment. Provide educators with the necessary knowledge and skills to implement equitable practices in their classrooms.

- **Coaching and Mentoring:** Pair educators with experienced mentors or instructional coaches who can provide guidance and support in implementing equitable assessment practices. Foster a culture of collaborative learning and reflection.

- **Collaborative Lesson Planning:** Encourage educators to engage in collaborative lesson planning sessions where they can share ideas, discuss assessment strategies, and explore ways to integrate equity into their instructional practices.

Cultivating a Reflective and Adaptive Mindset

To sustain equitable assessment practices, educators must cultivate a reflective and adaptive mindset. This involves regularly reflecting on their own biases, examining assessment practices, and making adjustments to ensure fairness and inclusivity. Strategies for cultivating a reflective and adaptive mindset include:

- **Self-Reflection:** Encourage educators to reflect on their own biases, assumptions, and beliefs about assessment. Provide opportunities for self-assessment and self-evaluation to identify areas for growth and improvement.

- **Data Analysis:** Use data to inform equitable assessment practices. Regularly analyze assessment results, identify patterns or disparities, and make informed decisions based on the data collected.

- **Continuous Improvement:** Encourage educators to embrace a growth mindset and seek opportunities for continuous improvement. Foster a culture of experimentation and innovation, where educators can try new approaches, evaluate their effectiveness, and make adjustments accordingly.

Sustaining equitable assessment practices requires a collective effort and ongoing commitment from all stakeholders involved in the educational community. By doing so, they contribute to a more inclusive and supportive educational environment where every student has the opportunity to thrive and succeed.

Conclusion

AS WE COME TO THE END of this book on proficiency scales and equitable grading, I find myself reflecting on the transformative power of these practices and the profound impact they can have on our educational systems. Throughout this journey, we have explored the fundamental concepts, practical strategies, and guiding principles that underpin this approach to assessment and grading. We have delved into the importance of promoting equity, student agency, and meaningful feedback in our classrooms.

By embracing proficiency scales, we have acknowledged the inherent value of focusing on student growth and development rather than solely relying on traditional letter grades. We have recognized the limitations of one-size-fits-all approaches to assessment and grading and have championed the need for personalized, targeted feedback that supports student progress. This shift in mindset and practice has the potential to revolutionize our educational landscapes and foster a culture of inclusion, collaboration, and continuous improvement.

Throughout this book, we have explored the vital role of educators as agents of change in creating equitable and empowering learning environments. We have seen how proficiency scales provide a framework for fair and accurate assessment, free from bias and stereotypes. We have learned how to design effective proficiency scales that align with equitable assessment practices and promote student success. We have discovered strategies for engaging students in their own assessment journey, fostering metacognition, reflection, and self-assessment skills.

Furthermore, we have examined the critical role of educators in addressing challenges, overcoming obstacles, and building supportive partnerships with parents and guardians. We have learned how to sustain equitable assessment practices over time and navigate the complex landscape of education with integrity and professionalism.

I would like to express my gratitude for joining me on this exploration of proficiency scales and equitable grading. It is my hope that this book has provided you with an understanding of these practices and has equipped you with the tools and inspiration to implement them in your own educational context.

Thank you, and best wishes on your continued journey toward equitable and effective assessment practices.

Further Reading

BROOKHART, SUSAN M. and Thomas R. Guskey, editors. *What We Know About Grading: What Works, What Doesn't, and What's Next.* ASCD, 2019.

Dueck, Myron. *Grading Smarter, Not Harder: Assessment Strategies That Motivate Kids and Help Them Learn.* ASCD, 2014.

Feldman, Joe. *Grading for Equity: What It Is, Why It Matters, and How It Can Transform Schools and Classrooms.* SAGE Publications, 2018.

Wexler, Natalie. *The Knowledge Gap: The Hidden Cause of America's Broken Education System—and How to Fix it*. Penguin Publishing Group, 2020.

Wormeli, Rick. *Fair Isn't Always Equal: Assessing & Grading in the Differentiated Classroom*. Stenhouse Publishers, 2006.

Don't miss out!

Visit the website below and you can sign up to receive emails whenever Cheryl Angst publishes a new book. There's no charge and no obligation.

https://books2read.com/r/B-A-SBAY-JCZJC

BOOKS 2 READ

Connecting independent readers to independent writers.

About the Author

Cheryl Angst has been teaching in the classroom for over twenty-five years. With a Masters in curriculum and instruction, her passion centers around finding tips, tricks, and strategies to enhance her practice.

Cheryl is a firm believer that learning should be fun for both the students and the teacher. If it isn't engaging, or doesn't spark joy, it's likely able to be done differently.

The "Quick Reads for Busy Educators" series is designed to maximize the precious time educators have. Each book is short enough to be read in an hour or less, but contains a wealth of information on the topic. Some books are overviews of strategies and approaches (enough to help educators decide if it's for them) and some are deeper dives into specific aspects of those larger approaches. This allows busy educators to grab the information they need quickly and efficiently.

If there's a topic you'd like to see covered in the "Quick Reads" series, please let us know!